My 7 Best Friends

by Eileen Maurer

Illustrated by
Gabrielle Gonzalez

I want to tell you about my 7 best friends.

I spend all of my time with these friends.

Together we make a great team.

Each of my friends plays a part in my life,
and out in the world.

They don't always agree on everything,
so I have to make sure they stay in touch
and communicate with each other.

It's very important to me to
keep my friends connected.

My 7 best
friends are...

my mind

my ears

my heart

my voice

my breath
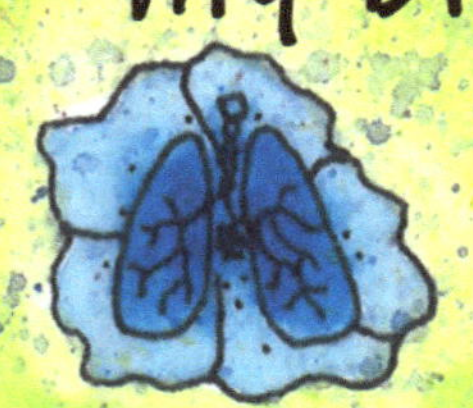

my hands
& feet

my eyes

My ears listen carefully to friends and family,

and leaders in the community,

and those in the news.

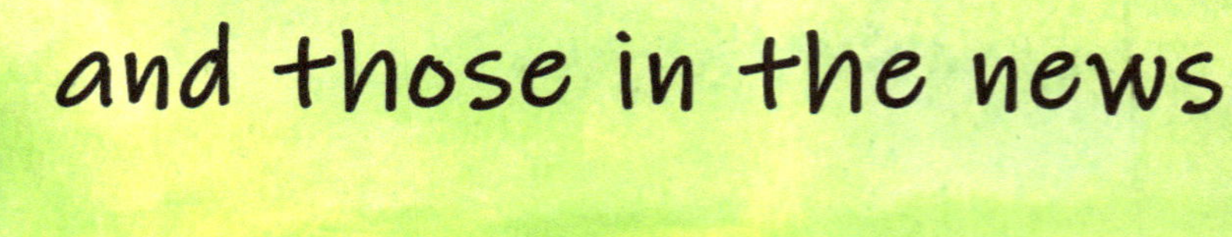

My eyes see what's going on in the lives of those close to me and those around the world.

My ears and eyes send information to my mind.

My mind helps make decisions about the truth in what I'm hearing and seeing.

My mind learns and grows from my experiences;
from the words and deeds of inspiring people,

from moral
and
religious
teachings,

and from
science
and
reasoning.

My mind opens my heart to
compassion, love, understanding, and justice.
Together my heart and mind build my beliefs.
My heart and mind help me decide how to respond.

My heart and mind tell me how
to serve in this world,
and send a call to action to my body.

I use my voice to talk to others,
to share thoughts and feelings,
to inform, discuss, support, encourage,
teach, laugh and sing.

My voice helps me speak out
against evil and injustice,
and speak up with others
who need to be heard.

My ears listen deeply to those in distress,
and my voice responds to help them feel better.

My hands reach out to offer love and support.

I gently squeeze their hands, or give them a hug
or put my arm around their shoulder.

My feet can take me to people, places,
animals and environments that
need extra help and loving care...

so that my hands can get busy
doing what needs to be done.

My feet can march in protest against injustice.

My feet get me outside in nature,
as often as possible,
to see and hear and feel all of the beauty on earth;
to remind me why I'm grateful to be alive...

even in the middle of tough times.

My most useful friend is my breath.

My breath keeps all my other friends connected.

when my heart breaks from sadness,
or my mind is confused and anxious,
my breath can shift their energy
and reset them ~

So my heart and mind
can encourage my eyes and ears,
my feet and hands,
and my voice,
to carry on.

As I get older, or when I'm sick,
or when I'm tired of trying so hard,
I find I am not always as strong as I want to be.

In those times, my heart and mind let me know
it's okay to rest...

take a break, be still, and just breathe.

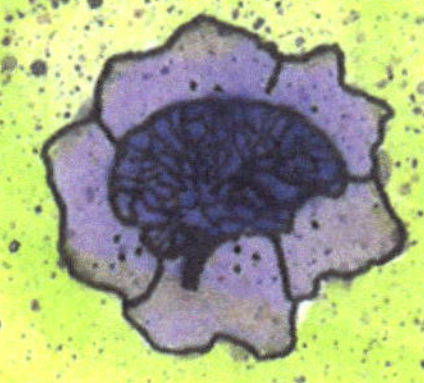

Not everyone has the same seven
friends that I do.
Some people have trouble using
their hands, or seeing, or hearing,
or walking, or speaking.
But they find a way to connect to
the world and make a difference.

Take a moment to think about your own best friends
and how you might put them into service in your life.
How will you use your...

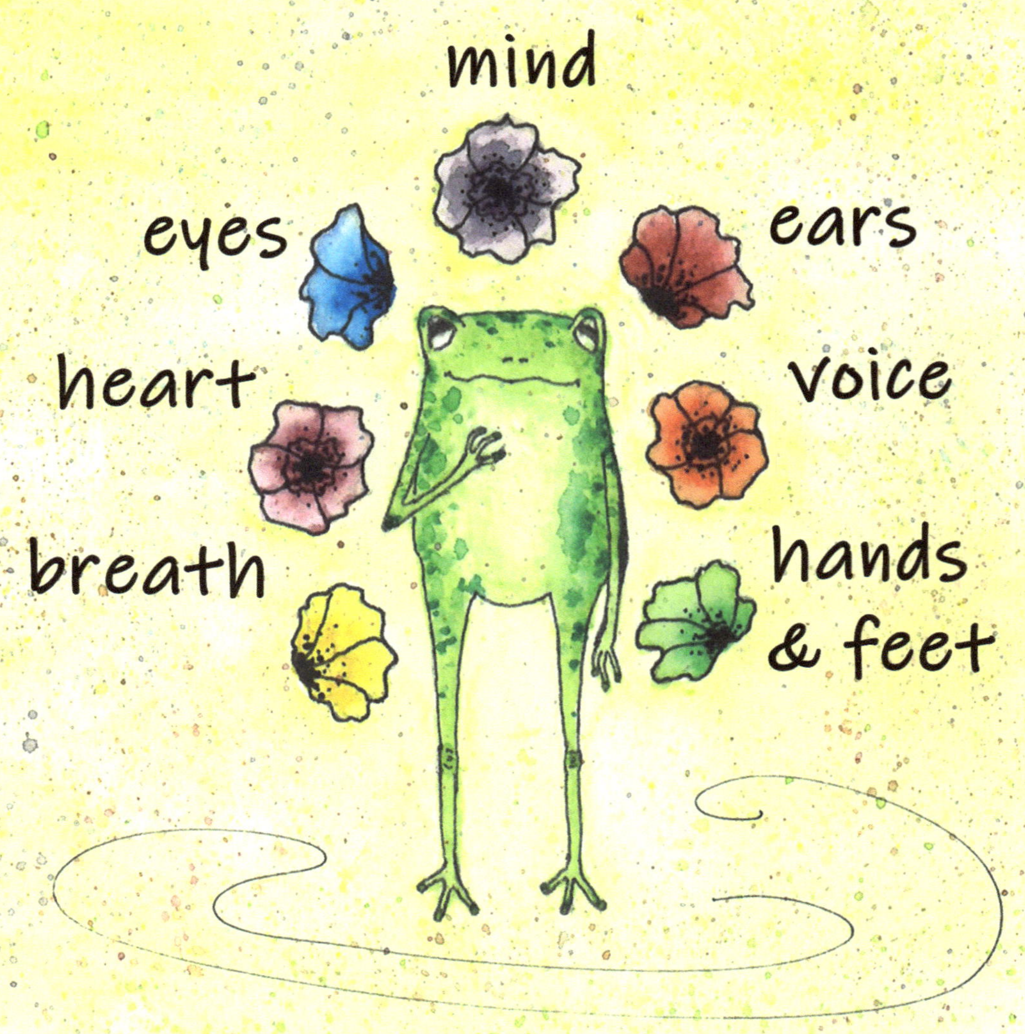